DATE DUE ОСТ 06

GAYLORD			PRINTED IN U.S.A.

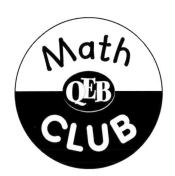

Math QEB Club

Adding and Subtracting Book 1

Ann Montague-Smith

QEB Publishing, Inc.

Published in the United States by
QEB Publishing, Inc.
23062 La Cadena Drive
Laguna Hills, CA 92653

www.qeb-publishing.com

Library of Congress Control Number: 2005921185

ISBN 1-59566-098-4

Written by Ann Montague-Smith
Designed and edited by The Complete Works
Illustrated by Peter Lawson
Photography by Steve Lumb

Publisher Steve Evans
Creative Director Louise Morley
Editorial Manager Jean Coppendale

Printed and bound in China

With thanks to:

Contents

I know all this!

You can make an addition sentence for the numbers on the red kite like this: 5+2=7. You can also make 2+5=7. Make two addition sentences for each kite.

You can also make 7−5=2 and 7−2=5. Make subtraction sentences for each kite.

4

Now try this

Work with a friend. One of you writes down a number sentence like 6+3=9. The other one writes down three other number sentences that use the same numbers. Now switch.

3+6=9
9−3=6
9−6=3

Missing numbers

You need a 1–6 dice, two counters, and a friend. Take turns to throw the dice. Move your counter to that number on the path. Now find the missing number in the number sentence. If you are correct, leave your counter where it is. If you are wrong, move your counter back to where you were before.

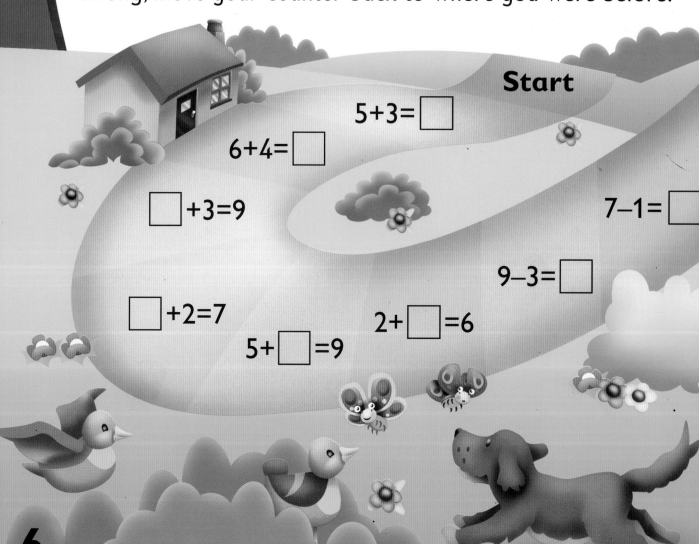

Start

$5+3=\square$

$6+4=\square$

$\square+3=9$

$7-1=\square$

$9-3=\square$

$\square+2=7$

$2+\square=6$

$5+\square=9$

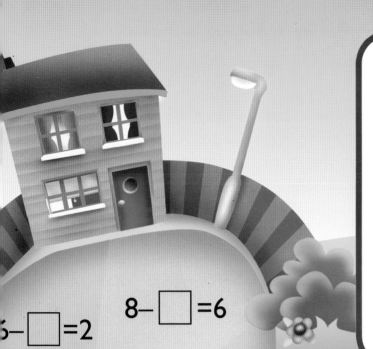

Now try this

What could go in the missing number boxes? Can you make five different number sentences?

$\square + \square = 8$.

Now try this.

$12 - \square = \square$

$8 - \square = 6$

$6 - \square = 2$

$6 - \square = 0$

$\square - 3 = 4$

$\square - 4 = 5$

$\square + 5 = 10$

$9 - \square = 2$

$6 - \square = 3$

Finish

Recognizing coins

Collect together 10 coins. Say their names. How many different sizes are there? How many different colors? Place a coin on each purse shown here.

How much is each coin worth?

8

Now try this

Which of your coins is worth the least?
Which is worth the most?
Now put your coins in order
of how much they are worth.

9

Paying at the store

You will need 10 coins. Decide which shoes you would like to buy and count out the pennies into the silver circles. How many pennies do you have left?

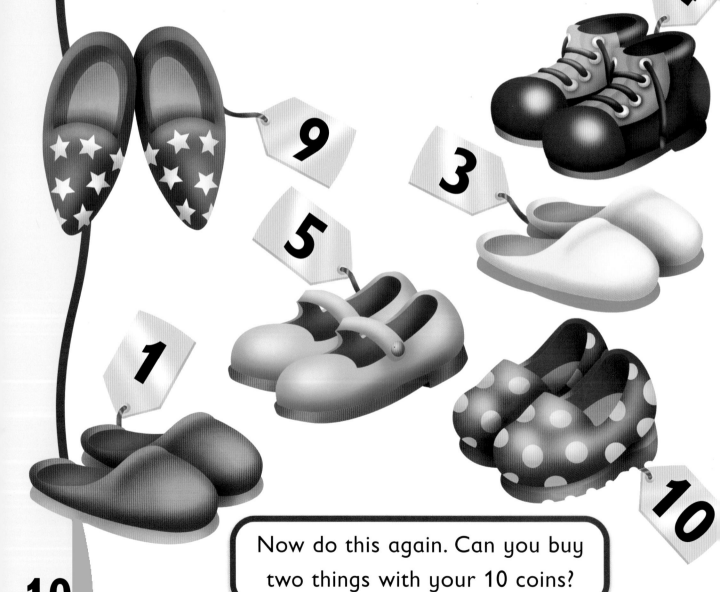

Now do this again. Can you buy two things with your 10 coins?

8

2

Challenge
Can you find three things to
buy with your 10 coins?
How many different ways
can you do this?

6

7

11

Giving change

Choose something to buy. Pick a coin to use, either the 10 or 20 one below. Work out how much change you will get by counting up from the price.

5

10

20

9

4

3

6

7

Buy two things this time. Choose a coin and work out your change.

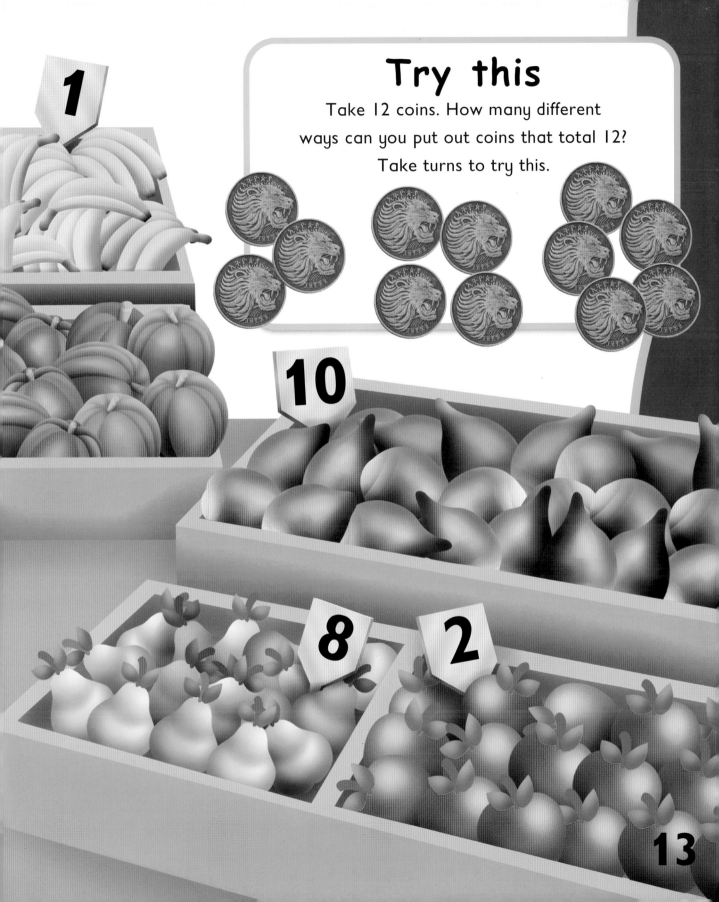

1

Try this

Take 12 coins. How many different
ways can you put out coins that total 12?
Take turns to try this.

10

8

2

13

Number game

You will need some counters and a friend. Choose two numbers between 1 and 10. Add your numbers together. Put a counter on the person below with the answer. If the number is already covered, you lose that turn. The winner is the one who covers the most people.

Can you find a way to cover every number?

14

Challenge

Choose three numbers between 1 and 10. Add two of the numbers together, then take away one of the numbers. Do this a few times.

$$4+5-1=8$$

15
18
19
4
3
8
12
10
17
5
7

A wormy problem

Some children measured these worms using buttons.
The difference in length between the two worms
was four buttons. How long could each worm be?

16

Now find five more lengths for each worm to be.

Challenge

Imagine that the difference in length between the worms is six coins. Find five lengths that each worm could be.

1 and 7

17

What's my number?

Read the clues. Find the number on the trophies.

14 **16** **17** **18** **19**

I am larger than 10
but smaller than 18.
I am even.
I am not 14.
What number am I?

I am not even.
I am less than 20
but more than 15.
I am the same as 8+9.
What number am I?

Tell someone how you found the answers.

I am even.
I am between
13 and 15.
What number am I?

Try this

With a friend, take turns to think
of a number. Think of some clues.
Say your clues to your friend.
Can they find out your number?

My number
is less than 9.
My number is
not even.

5?

I am not a double.
I am between 15 and 20.
I am not 17.
What number am I?

I am a double.
I am larger than 16.
I am smaller than 20.
What number am I?

1

Kittens in baskets

You will need 20 counters or coins. These are your kittens. The kittens have been naughty. While their mothers were not looking, they sneaked out of their baskets. Can you put them back? Each basket can have any even number of kittens in it.

Can you find another way to do this?

Challenge

Can you put the kittens into the baskets so that each basket has an odd number of kittens? Find another way to do this.

Supporting notes

I know all this!, pages 4–5

If children know, or can quickly recall, one addition or subtraction fact, then they can deduce three other facts. If children aren't confident about this, write down one of the facts like this: $6+3=9$. Then ask, "What is $3+6$? What do you notice? So what is $9-3$? And $9-6$? Now what do you notice?" If children find the calculation difficult, count together, using a mental or real number line.

Missing numbers, pages 6–7

If children are not sure how to find out what is missing for $2+\boxed{}=6$, discuss how they can count on from 2, in ones, to 6. Then ask, "Is this true, $2+4=6$?" For subtraction, try counting up like this: for $9-\boxed{}=2$, count on from the 2 to the 9. Ask, "Is this true $9-7=2$?"

Recognizing coins, pages 8–9

Encourage children to group real coins and name them. Separate the coins by their color, so all the copper/silver coins are together. Discuss how you can recognize each coin by size and color, and by the presidents' heads on the coins' faces.

Paying at the store, pages 10–11

Use the lowest value coins for simple calculations. Encourage children to count the pennies out, one at a time, until they have enough to buy the items. In cases where they are "buying" two items, encourage them to total the two amounts mentally, and then count out the correct number of coins.

Giving change, pages 12–13

Help children understand the method of giving change by counting up. Explain that you need to count up from the price to the amount of money that you give, like this: "4 and 5, 6, 7, 8, 9, 10. I counted 6, so the change is 6."

Number game, pages 14–15

This game encourages children to total pairs of numbers mentally. If children find this hard, discuss the strategies that they could use, such as doubling, near doubles (double and add one), and counting on in ones from the larger number.

A wormy problem, pages 16–17

This problem is about the difference between pairs of numbers. If the children find this challenging, begin with the number 1 and ask, "What number would be 4 more than 1? Yes, 5. So the difference between 5 and 1 is 4." Then try 4 more than 2, so that the children begin to see a pattern forming of 1, 5; 2, 6; 3, 7; etc.

What's my number?, pages 18–19

Read the clues together. Discuss each one, and ask, "What does it tell you?" If children are unsure about odd and even numbers, count from 0 to 20 in twos, and agree that these are the even numbers. Now do the same for counting in twos starting on 1, and agree that these are the odd numbers.

Kittens in baskets, pages 20–21

Children will explore adding four small even numbers to make 20. Begin by counting in twos from 0 to 20 to remind the children of the even numbers. There are many different ways to put the kittens back in their baskets. For example: 4, 6, 4, 6; 8, 2, 8, 2; 2, 4, 6, 8; etc. Odd numbers are possible, too: 5, 5, 5, 5; 9, 1, 9, 1; etc. If the original puzzle is too hard, begin with 10 counters, so that the kittens go into their baskets like this: 2, 2, 2, 4. This is the only solution. Now try 20 kittens.

23

Using this book

The illustrations in this book are bright, cheerful, and colorful, and are designed to capture children's interest. Sit somewhere comfortable together as you look at the book. Children of this age will usually need to have the instructional words on the pages read to them. Please read these to them, then encourage them to take part in the activity.

The activities in this book invite the children to use what they know about addition, subtraction, and properties of numbers, such as odd and even numbers. Totals for addition are up to 20, and subtraction is within 0 to 10. For addition, children will be beginning to use strategies such as counting on in ones from the larger number, such as 8+5: 9, 10, 11, 12, 13. So 8+5=13. Similarly, counting on, or back, can be used for subtraction, or for finding the difference between two numbers. For example, 8–5. To find the difference between 5 and 8, count up from 5 to 8: 6, 7, 8. Three numbers have been counted so, 8–5=3. At first, children may find it useful to use a number line. Encourage them to progress to counting mentally along a number line that they imagine in their heads. They may like to check how many numbers they count with their fingers.

Encourage children to explain how they solved the problems. Being able to explain their thinking, and to use the correct mathematical vocabulary, helps children clarify in their minds what they have just done. Also, where there are children who are not as sure how to solve a problem, hearing how the others did it, and the techniques they used, helps them to use these methods more effectively.

At this stage, children will be beginning to write number sentences, using +, –, and =. Encourage lots of practice. It is a way of recording what's been done, and it can clarify the meanings of abstract signs.

Above all, enjoy the mathematical games, activities, and challenges in this book together.